POCKET DORCHESTER

Chris Shaw

With illustrations by Graham Shaw

S. B. PUBLICATIONS
SEAFORD, SUSSEX

By the same author
The Dorset Garden Guide
Dorset for Free

First published in 1997 by S. B. Publications,
c/o 19 Grove Road, Seaford, East Sussex BN25 1TP

©1997 Chris Shaw

All rights reserved. No part of this publication may be reproduced, stored
in a retrieval system or transmitted in any form or by any means,
electronic, mechanical, photocopying, recording or otherwise,
without the prior permission of the publisher
and copyright holder.

ISBN 1 85770 129 1

Designed and typeset by CGB, Lewes
Printed by MFP Design and Print
Longford Trading Estate, Thomas Street,
Stretford, Manchester M32 0JT

CONTENTS

	Page
INTRODUCTION	4
DORCHESTER, THE HISTORY	5
1 THE COLLITON WALK	9
2 MILL STREAM MEANDER	16
3 SOUTH STREET STROLL	21
4 FINDING FORDINGTON	27
5 ON THE EDGE OF TOWN	31
DETAILS OF MUSEUMS AND PLACES TO VISIT	32

Front cover: Dorchester from the River Frome and water meadows.
Title page: The town centre, seen from Salisbury Fields.
Back cover: The Georgian elegance of Fordington High Street.

ABOUT THE AUTHOR

Chris Shaw moved to Dorset from Hampshire in the early 1980s and fell immediately under the spell of her adoptive county. She has immersed herself in its history and topography and now, as part of a husband and wife team – architect Graham does the expert illustrations – devotes as much time as possible from her secretarial day job to communicating her interest in Dorset to readers.

INTRODUCTION

VISITORS to the county town of Dorset, whether arriving by car, coach or train, need only their feet to explore it for part of Dorchester's charm is its compact size. Happily it has not overspilled into the surrounding farmland and water meadows as have so many other county towns.

Here are details of four walks, each covering a distinct area of Dorchester. Places and items of interest are pointed out, their history recounted and there are many illustrations. Each walk has its own street map on which the position of places mentioned in the text are indicated by numbers. All walks start at the Town Pump, Cornhill, the very heart of Dorchester. It is starred on each map. A walk can be followed in its entirety or part-explored, depending on the time available.

This guide is meant to whet the appetite rather than answer every single question. It covers major points of interest and on occasions takes a look at some of the lighter moments in the town's development.

Painted on the wall inside the Corn Exchange are the words written about the county town of Dorset by Daniel Defoe on his travels around the British Isles in the eighteenth century. Of it he said: 'A man . . . might as agreeably spend his time, and as well, in Dorchester, as in any town I know in England.'

So welcome to Dorchester – and I hope you enjoy the walks.

Chris Shaw
Charminster
Dorchester
May 1997

DORCHESTER

Dorchester. We come to it twenty centuries after Christ, and find it one of England's most delightful towns with sights that hold us spellbound.
(Arthur Mee. The King's England - Dorset)

THE history of Dorchester begins on its south-western outskirts in the parish of Winterborne St Martin, where the grassy ramparts of Maiden Castle rise to form probably the most impressive earthworks in the country. It is a great afternoon stroll around the perimeter of this ancient feat of civil engineering that owes nothing to mechanical earth-movers and teams of college-bred professionals and to whose lowest slopes Dorchester has spread.

Mai Dun began as a small Neolithic earthwork about 3,900 BC, shaped using the most primitive of tools. It is considered unlikely that the early site was a settlement, but was perhaps used for important tribal ceremonies. Over the next 4,000 years it was in turn enlarged, inhabited, deserted – at one stage it was even covered by trees.

By 100 BC Mai Dun was populated again, the tribal centre of the *Durotriges*. Further embankments with staggered entrances had been added to fortify the site, which housed a large community. These *dwellers near water* had moved north and west across Europe, finding a route inland along the Frome valley from Wareham while looking for a place to settle.

Their peaceful, mainly agricultural, way of life was savagely shattered in 43 AD. Where small, nomadic groups had led, the might of the Empire followed. The invading Romans contemptuously swept aside the defences of Maiden Castle, laying claim to a wide area. Graves have been excavated on the massive hillfort of people who met their death in violent and bloody battle. Many artefacts found particularly during the 1930s are now displayed in the Dorset County Museum, including the famous skeleton with an arrow-head lodged in its spine.

Within twenty years of invading the Romans had laid out and begun to construct a new town at a point where a major crossing of the River Frome was probably already established and evidence of timber buildings dating from 60-70 AD has come to light. Longer-lasting building materials followed as the newcomers settled in. The stone footings of the villa in Colliton Park are of a spacious Roman home. The rooms had fine mosaic floors, at least one of which was a hypocaust, a suspended floor with heating below. Public baths were laid out in the centre of town, where they were uncovered this century during excavations for redevelopment and car parking.

The baths, heating systems and, probably, decorative fountains, were all served by water channelled in by aqueduct. This was cut through the ancient defences of Poundbury, a hillfort on the north-western corner of Dorchester. Engineering techniques perfected in Europe brought fresh water from higher up the Frome valley into the growing town of Durnovaria, the large clay-lined channel evidence of the intended long-term nature of the Roman occupation. Its route can still be seen like a grass shelf, where it runs along both sides of the Dorchester bypass which cuts through Fordington Bottom from the Bridport Road to the Wolfeton roundabout.

By the beginning of the fifth century the Roman army had been recalled to Europe. Their descendants, now firmly established and trading in such as Purbeck marble and local pottery, faced an increasing Saxon presence. These were truly Dark Ages, when even the pages of history bear scant paragraphs of information. By the eighth century the settling Saxons were themselves under pressure from the long-ships of Norway. Vikings landed on the Dorset coast in 789 AD, killing the King's Reeve who had intercepted their arrival in the hopes of honest trade. Reeve, or mayor, was a royal appointment, so the town already had considerable status. The name of Dorset as a county was recorded in 880 AD.

Following the Conquest in 1066, buildings using local stone were soon establishing the permanence of Norman possession, in particular the churches of St Peter's, All Saints and Holy Trinity. These three parishes with their medieval streets set the pattern for central Dorchester which is still evident, with only the main east-west and north-south axes possibly echoing the Roman plan aligned on the positions of the old town gates. The town, which was almost completely surrounded by lands belonging to the village of Fordington, remained inside its Roman walls. As they fell into decay their stone was used on repairs and new buildings and by the sixteenth century they had disappeared, leaving only banks and ditches to mark the town boundary.

Medieval and Elizabethan eras gave way to the rigid disciplines of the Puritans and the Civil War. The Reverend John White came to Dorchester as rector of Holy Trinity and St Peter's from 1606 to 1648, preaching hell-fire and damnation to a reluctant congregation. It was a turbulent century which, as it approached its last quarter, brought the name of Dorchester to everyone's lips for it was one of the places at which Judge Jeffreys

The South Walks

presided over what came to be known as the Bloody Assizes at which the Monmouth rebels were tried after their defeat at the Battle of Sedgemoor.

The numbers of thatched buildings gradually declined as all-too-frequent fires of the period took their toll. The Georgians rebuilt and enlarged the town with elegant houses, their windows distinctively paned and bowed. The Roman banks and ditches were transformed into the tree-lined promenades known as the Walks and by the time Queen Victoria was crowned the Dorchester street scene had become much as it is today.

The town's prosperity was boosted by travellers from further afield. It had several good inns and in the 1830s, at the height of the coaching era,

Dorchester was stage for nearly fifty arrivals and departures every week.

It changed with the arrival of the railway in 1847, bringing holidaymakers from London on their way to the seaside resort of Weymouth. While Castleman and Brunel argued over which was the better gauge, it was proposed that further track to Weymouth could be laid straight through the centre of Maumbury Rings.

The Rings, like Mai Dun, has been used for large gatherings since Neolithic times. As a Roman amphitheatre it held displays of prowess, with wild animals and gladiators pitted against each other. During the Civil War it was fortified and occupied by troops. Even as late as the Victorian era, a public execution or national celebration could attract crowds of up to ten thousand within the grassy banks. Thankfully a strenuous appeal by local historians and archaeologists of the Dorset Field Club brought about a change of policy and prevented part of Dorchester's ancient history becoming railway sidings.

The twentieth century has brought an increased awareness of the importance of conservation. The demolition of existing buildings and the erection of new can still raise the temperature and Dorchester, like many other towns, is trying to balance the needs of newcomers, shoppers and tourists with the preferences of long-established residents.

The new 'village' of Poundbury, the vision of Prince Charles, is already spreading to the line of the western bypass. However, limits have been defined. Even when this expansion is complete Dorchester will remain small, its borders merging gently into farmland and water-meadows, keeping the town as one with the county at large.

1 THE COLLITON WALK

The view east through central Dorchester.

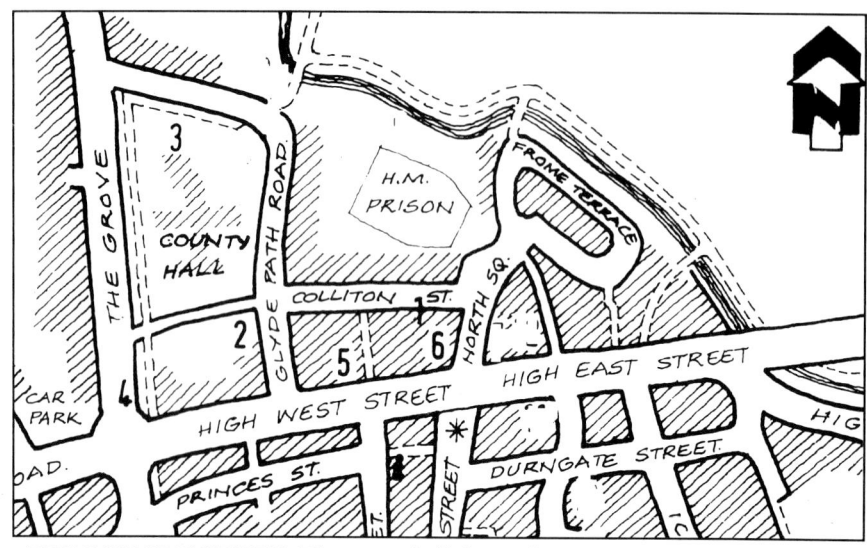

THE COLLITON WALK. The start of all the walks is the Town Pump which is indicated on the map with a star ✳. Numbered points of interest are: 1 John White's rectory, 2 Colliton House, 3 Roman town house, 4 Thomas Hardy's statue, 5 Old Crown Court,

THE hub of Dorchester has always been Cornhill, dividing South Street from North Square, where High East Street becomes High West Street. Here was the octagonal Cupola, a small meeting room on pillars over market space below. Increasingly busy streets led to this being demolished in the late eighteenth century. Its position is marked by the Town Pump, (starred on the above map) once described as 'the Arc de Triomphe of Dorchester . . . very large, very parochial looking and very self-conscious', which was erected to replace a well further down South Street.

When the Cupola was demolished, an imposing Guildhall was built right across the entrance to North Square with traffic passing underneath. This in turn was replaced by the present Town Hall in 1847. The Corn Exchange and distinctive clock tower were added in the 1860s, the latter partly financed by Alderman Galpin. Since the clock had no apparent means of support, locals referred to it as Galpin's Folly and waited for it to collapse.

Walk into North Square, once known as Bull Stake, with St Peter's Church on your left. Note the old carved stone nameplate to POLICE STATION AND MARKETS on the Corn Exchange wall. Ahead is the entrance to the prison, where the road curves right and down to the mill stream of the River Frome.

Colliton Street, or Pease Lane to give it the old name, is a quaint collection of cottages. Walk along towards the antique market which has an ever-changing stock and a bargain or two for those with time to explore.

Look for **John White's Rectory (1)**, with its commemorative plaque. The Reverend John White, rector of Holy Trinity and St Peter's from 1606 to 1648, was known as the Patriarch of Dorchester. His strict Puritan beliefs resulted in fiery sermons, encouraging his congregations to be God-fearing and stay away from Dorchester beer.

He was instrumental in the emigration of one group of Puritans to America, persuading King Charles I to sign the necessary charter for those who eventually settled in New Dorchester, near Boston, Massachusetts. The church there is still known as the Daughter of John White. A fourteenth century arch removed from the cottage during alterations is set incongruously inside Superdrug in South Street. The plaque on the rectory makes interesting reading, especially the reputed visitation by the Devil.

Colliton Street ends at Glyde Path Road with **Colliton House (2)** immediately ahead. Until the late 1930s, this house stood in extensive grounds sweeping down to the mill stream on the northern edge of town. It was all purchased by Dorset County Council in 1920, Colliton Park being now almost covered by County Hall and the Library. Excavations for the new buildings uncovered some of the oldest in Dorchester; the remains of six Roman town houses, at least one of which had boasted a verandah supported on stone columns subsequently retrieved from ten metres down a nearby well.

Mosaic floors which were covered up for safe-keeping once those excavations were completed have now been cleared again and a lightweight protective structure erected over, to reflect the size of the original building. Further conservation work has been undertaken on the Roman walls including the reinstatement of a window. An information centre is planned as part of further development of the site. The best way to reach the **Roman House (3)** is to walk north, down the hill and bear left into North Walk. There is a gate clearly marked behind County Hall.

Leave by the same gate and continue along North Walk past Northernhay, where it links with Colliton Walk. Here you can appreciate the height of the old Roman banks and walls around Dorchester. The Grove takes traffic out of town along what was the ditch at the foot of the bank, while the flint walls towered on top. The 'green walls', as the remains of the Roman defences used to be known, were planted with limes and sycamores nearly two hundred years ago. Replacements have been made including horse chestnuts which are a magnificent sight when they are in flower.

At Top o' Town is this statue of **Thomas Hardy (4)**, whose beautifully descriptive novels of Wessex are still in demand worldwide. He was born in 1840 at Higher Bockhampton, just east of Dorchester, and spent his early working years learning the profession of architecture with John Hicks whose practice was at the lower end of South Street.

Hardy and his father played in the band of the church of St Michael's, Stinsford, a stone's throw away from the cottage where he was born, and the characters of these hamlets and their inhabitants provided local colour for his books. The novelist left the area for many years but returned when in his mid forties to build Max Gate, on the Wareham Road. There he lived until his death in 1928.

The statue was sculpted by Eric Kennington at the suggestion of T E Lawrence (of Arabia) who was a friend of the Hardys and a frequent visitor at Max Gate. Kennington had illustrated Lawrence's book, *The Seven Pillars of Wisdom*. The statue was unveiled by Sir James Barrie, creator of Peter Pan, also a close friend of Hardy. It was he who carried Hardy's ashes to London for burial in Poets' Corner at Westminster Abbey. Hardy's heart remains in his much loved countryside, Stinsford churchyard.

Turning left to descend through town, note the Old Tea House with its date of 1635. The view ahead is probably the one most associated with Dorchester. The tower of St Peter's, the Town Hall clock and the soaring spire of All Saints are an instantly recognisable street scene. High West Street has many interesting houses with impressive entrances. Look above the more modern shop fronts to the upper storeys with bow windows, Georgian sashes, elaborate carvings and other architectural details.

An oddity in this Dorset town is the Tutankhamun Exhibition. It is the only one outside Egypt dedicated to the boy pharoah and includes a reconstruction of the tomb complete with mummy and gold mask.

The first turning on the left is Glyde Path Road, with the old name of Shirehall Lane still painted up above eye level. Thomas Hardy lived in the lane while he designed and built Max Gate.

Shire Hall was home to the Dorset County Council before it moved downhill to Stratton House – now West Dorset District Council offices – and then into Colliton Park. It was at Shire Hall that the county's store of gunpowder was kept under lock and key. In the great fire of 1613, which tore the heart out of the town, destroying about three hundred houses and two churches, the barrels of explosives were smothered in wet rags and rolled out into the countryside for safety. Had there been an explosion in the store the scale of the damage would have been beyond imagining.

Shire Hall was rebuilt in 1638 and again, as it stands today in Portland stone, in 1796. It incorporates the **Old Crown Court (5)** where the Tolpuddle Martyrs were tried in 1834 'for the founding of rural trade unionism'. The building is marked by the bronze plaque pictured right.

After the introduction of the Corn Laws in the early nineteenth century, the price for Dorset grain plummeted. Land owners tried to reduce their costs still further by turning to mechanisation, leaving already poorly paid farm workers in danger of having no work at all.

The Tolpuddle men, headed by George Loveless, formed a society to try and improve their situation but met with dreadful consequences. They were sentenced to seven years transportation to Australia. Following a public outcry the men were pardoned in 1836 but endured much hardship and cruelty before finally returning home. The Old Crown Court was bought by the TUC in 1956 and opened as a memorial to them.

Today it looks exactly as it did in 1834 and the cells, both old and new, can also be seen.

Carved on the Shire Hall wall are the distances to Blandford, Bridport and Hyde Park Corner. Opposite is the Ship Inn, reputedly Dorchester's oldest hostelry. It dates from the seventeenth century as does the nearby Royal Oak.

Take a look at 13 High West Street, opposite Stratton House, with its narrow black and white facade. The shop front has remained unchanged for more than a century. It used to be owned by William Gibbs, 'hairdresser, perfumer and peruke maker'.

On the corner of Trinity Street, above eye-level, is the name stone of Genges, a nineteenth century firm which began on the site of Davis and Sons Soda Water Manufactory. On the other corner, the Horse with the Red Umbrella used to be J T Godwin's Glass and China shop, behind which was the Loyalty Theatre which opened with a fanfare in 1828. It was purpose-built with stage, dressing rooms, green room and a gallery supported by fluted and painted posts. Despite the enthusiasm with which it was received, in less than ten years the theatre had closed. The building was finally demolished, to public dismay, in 1965.

Holy Trinity Roman Catholic Church has been rebuilt several times over the centuries. There was a medieval church on the site that was seriously damaged by the 1613 fire. It was replaced by a simple building with a plain west tower but in 1824 this was taken down and rebuilt in fanciful Gothic style.

The present church was erected in 1876 to a design by Benjamin Ferrey, who was also responsible for the Corn Exchange.

Opposite the church, Judge Jeffreys' and the shop next door have timber-framed Tudor frontages. The judge is said to have lodged in one of these houses while presiding over the infamous Bloody Assizes at which those who took part in the ill-fated Monmouth rebellion of 1685 were sentenced.

James, Duke of Monmouth, had landed at Lyme Regis to contest the throne of his uncle, James II but the uprising he led was short-lived and his followers soon brought to justice. The hearings took place in the Oak Room of the Antelope Hotel in Cornhill, the assize sermon being read in St Peter's Church, as it still is today. The head of a rebel was impaled on a spike by the church porch to reinforce the severity of the offences about to be tried.

The Dorset County Museum was built in 1883 on the site of the old

George Inn and is the headquarters of the Dorset Natural History and Archaeological Society.

William Barnes, 1801–1886, was one of the society's founders, concerned with others that 'the disturbance of the surface of the county in the formation of railroads' would uncover much historical evidence which would be lost if some method of recording and safe-keeping was not put in hand.

He was born near Sturminster Newton, and had a chequered career as schoolmaster and cleric during which he became a skilled linguist and famed dialect poet. His statue stands outside St Peter's Church – in frockcoat and knee breeches, apparently his standard wear as he strode around the town.

St Peter's (6) was a Norman church and the Norman archway inside the porch is the earliest stonework in town, apart from a small section of Roman wall. The building is now substantially fifteenth century and was restored in the 1850s by Dorchester architect John Hicks and his pupil, the young Thomas Hardy. The Reverend John White, whose rectory you saw in Colliton Street, is buried under the porch. It is believed that he preached from the fine seventeenth century pulpit that is still in use today.

Once outside St Peter's again, you are within sight of the Town Pump and your starting point.

The Old Tea House bears the date 1635

2 MILL STREAM MEANDER

The mill stream on the River Frome.

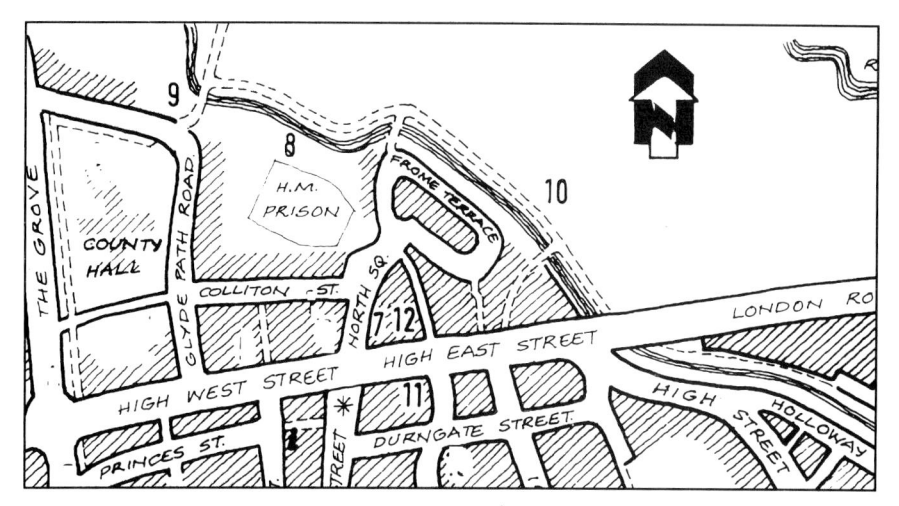

MILL STREAM MEANDER. Start from the ✻. Numbered points of interest are:
7 Corn Exchange. 8 Mill stream. 9 Hangman's Cottage. 10 Riverside reserve.
11 All Saints Church. 12 King's Arms.

THIS begins, like the Colliton Walk, by crossing from the top of South Street and the Town Pump into North Square. Notice the old name of The Bow on the St Peter's Church corner.

On the right hand corner is the **Corn Exchange** and **Town Hall (7)**. The latter was originally built over an open market space below, with the Corn Exchange added at the rear in the 1860s to a design by Benjamin Ferrey, the same architect who remodelled Holy Trinity Church in High West Street.

Walk past Colliton Street and downhill to the right, towards the mill stream of the River Frome. This high bluff overlooking the water-meadows was the site of a castle built soon after the Norman Conquest. It was under attack during the civil wars that marred the reign of Stephen from 1135 to 1154; was used as a headquarters by King John; and was still undergoing repairs and refurbishments late in the thirteenth century.

The County Gaol, built on the old castle site in the late eighteenth century, was the fourth of five prisons in town. The first stood on the corner of Icen Way, or Gaol Lane as it used to be called, which led to the scaffold in South Walks. Two in succession were then built at the bottom of High East Street where the pretty Casterbridge Hotel now stands. The fifth is the austere red brick Victorian building of today. Only a Portland stone gateway on the river side remains of the eighteenth century building. It can just be seen from the mill stream path.

North Square was the site of Dorchester's first purpose-built theatre, near the end of Friary Lane. It was built at the request of Henry Lee, manager of the Salisbury Company of Comedians, who regularly brought a touring company to town. In 1813 a new player, Edmund Kean, joined Lee's company in Dorchester. Kean's acting so impressed a visiting London manager that he was offered a contract and the man who came to be known as 'the greatest tragedian of his time' made his biggest career move ever, from Dorchester's tiny theatre to Drury Lane. A later theatre was built behind the Horse with the Red Umbrella, once J T Godwin's Glass and China Shop, in Trinity Street.

Note Chubb's Almshouse of 1822 before you leave North Square to walk down Friary Hill to the site of Friary Mill, one of a dozen listed at Domesday. By the mid fifteenth century it seems only the site remained. It was owned by Sir John Byconil who had been knighted by Henry Tudor for his valiant part in the Battle of Bosworth Field. In gratitude at his monarch's recognition he gave the mill site to Franciscans and was to be admitted as one of their founders provided he first re-established a mill, or mills, on the River Frome for them. Forty shillings of the mill profits every year were to be put aside in a triple-locked chest, to ensure their upkeep. For his own salvation the knight was to be prayed for by name every week and the brother saying the prayer was to receive six pence.

Friary Mill survived the destruction of the Friary in 1536 and was still operating as a corn and saw mill at the beginning of this century, the last miller being Joshua Allen. The tail race in front of Frome Terrace was filled in about 1902.

To make a short detour, cross the bridge over the **mill stream (8)** and turn left. The path leads to picturesque **Hangman's Cottage (9)** where you can turn north to the Blue Bridge over the River Frome which flows several hundred yards away.

The main route takes you in front of Frome Terrace, one of the most popular groups of small houses in Dorchester, facing onto the mill stream. Follow round the end of the terrace towards the Orchard Street sign, but take the rough path through a narrow gateway between the sign and Greenings Court.

This leads through the now deserted Mariners Parade, the site of the old Eldridge brewery, and back to High East Street. Turn left and a few yards away you will find the ornate brick archway that leads into Greenings

Court, an unexpected group of old cottages tucked away from the main hustle and bustle. At the bottom of Greenings Court is another small footbridge over the mill stream, where the tannery used to be.

Turn left and you will find a small nature trail by the mill stream with a board walk to keep your feet dry. The wetland habitat of the **Riverside Reserve (10)** attracts butterflies, beetles and other insects. Rose bay willowherb, comfrey and reeds cover the wettest areas while shrubs and small trees provide cover for a variety of birds including nuthatch, finches, willow and sedge warbler, robin and tits.

After crossing the bridge turn right along a path to rejoin High East Street where it becomes London Road. Here the mill stream travels underneath the Swan Bridge through to Fordington.

Opposite is the old Lott and Walne iron foundry where the ornate clock in the Borough Gardens was cast as well as more utilitarian items such as the hatches on the River Frome that control the flow of water through the water-meadows.

Turn uphill from this point and follow High East Street back towards The Bow. E Channon and Sons, is the successor to Channons Carriage and Motor Works where, in 1905, the first motorcar to be made in Dorset was designed and produced. The all-British Channon was a ten horsepower four seater which sold for 260 guineas.

Just past the brick archway into Greenings Court, Icen Way (the old Gaol Lane) is on the left, then the soaring spire of **All Saints Church (11)**. This was one of the three medieval churches in Dorchester but, like the others, suffered fire damage and underwent subsequent rebuildings. The present edifice, with its spire, was built in 1845 at a cost of £3,000. The church is now deconsecrated and used as a store by the Dorset County Museum.

The road leads uphill past the pillared entrance and lovely bow windows of the **King's Arms (12)**, one of Dorchester's old coaching inns. Like the Antelope in Cornhill it was rebuilt and enlarged in the early nineteenth century when coaching traffic was at its height and was the setting for a celebration dinner in Thomas Hardy's *The Mayor of Casterbridge*.

From here the Town Pump, the start of the walk, is a few steps away.

The sluice gates on the mill stream

3 SOUTH STREET STROLL

The ornate Hansford Clock in the Borough Gardens was cast in the Lott and Walne foundry at Fordington which closed in 1932.

SOUTH STREET STROLL.

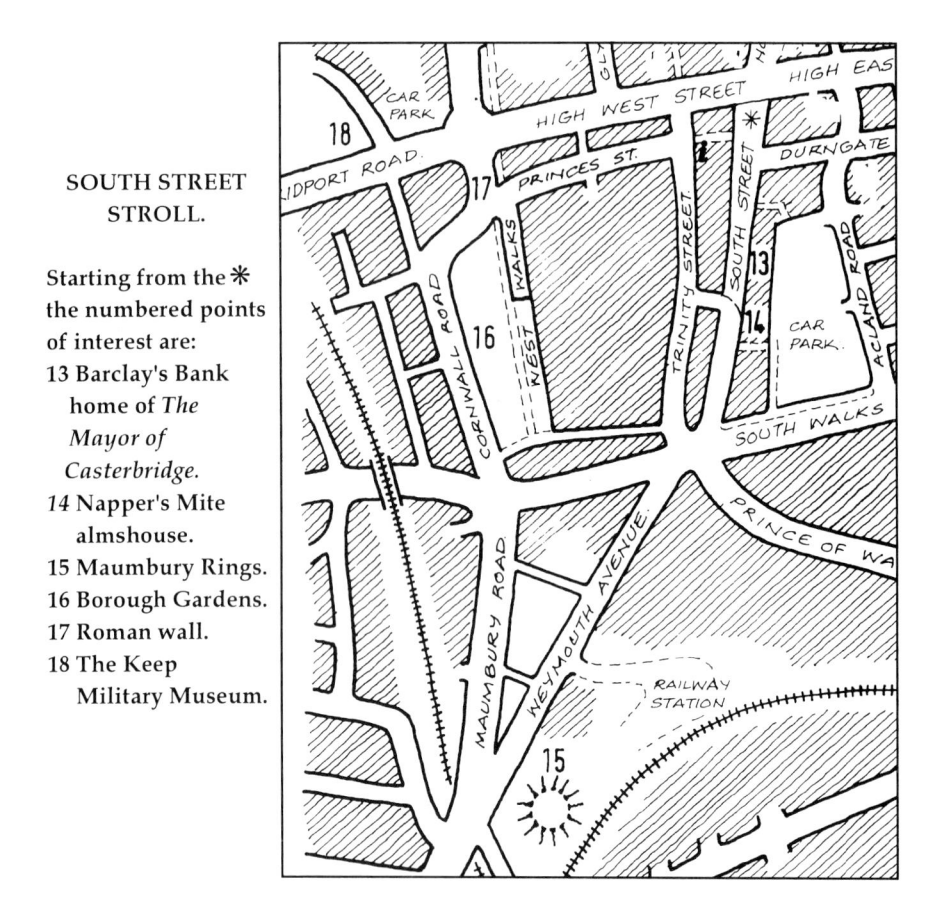

Starting from the ✶ the numbered points of interest are:
13 Barclay's Bank home of *The Mayor of Casterbridge.*
14 Napper's Mite almshouse.
15 Maumbury Rings.
16 Borough Gardens.
17 Roman wall.
18 The Keep Military Museum.

SOUTH STREET, with the Town Pump marking its wider northern end known as Cornhill, is now Dorchester's main shopping area. Until the nineteenth century it was mainly residential, trading taking place in the High Streets, but gradually the beautifully proportioned windows and doors of Georgian houses were replaced with the vacant stares of wide display windows. Upper storeys and roofs still have small balconies, dormers, fine detailing and mouldings over some of the less attractive retail outlets.

Antelope Walk is an arcade of shops. Judge Jeffreys' Bloody Assizes of 1685 were held in the Oak Room of the old inn, now a tea room, when King James II punished rebels who had supported the Duke of Monmouth in his bid for the crown of England at the Battle of Sedgemoor. More than three hundred were put on trial in three different areas. Seventy four were sent to the gallows and nearly two hundred transported. The Antelope was one of Dorchester's thriving coaching inns and was rebuilt in the early nineteenth century to cope with the increasing numbers of travellers. More than three dozen coaches every week covered the roads between Dorchester and Weymouth, Exeter, Bristol, Bath, Southampton, Portsmouth and London.

Opposite, 8 Cornhill was the home of Sir Frederick Treves, surgeon to Queen Victoria and founder of the Red Cross. As a boy he watched his father run a successful furniture business, but grew up to pioneer surgery on the appendix.

Further down on the left is Tudor Arcade, on the site of the Greyhound Inn and Yard. There was once a Nonconformist school here, one pupil being the young Thomas Hardy. At the end of the arcade is Waitrose and, on the left, an arch which belonged to the Greyhound Inn and which has survived several moves due to various redevelopments. By the arch are modern panels in relief showing some of the history of Dorchester. They were erected when the supermarket was built.

During that redevelopment twenty-one huge post holes each about a metre square were discovered, forming an arc which looked as though it had originally been part of a complete circle. If so, the circle would have been about 275 metres in diameter. This massive structure, whatever it was, dates from about 2,750 BC. The positions of the post holes are now marked in red on the floor of Waitrose's basement car park.

Back in South Street continue walking away from the Pump and keep your eyes open for **Barclays Bank (13).** The building used to be the handsome home of a solicitor and was described by Hardy as the Mayor's house in *The Mayor of Casterbridge*. It is one of the more attractive of the old buildings.

Marks and Spencer occupies the site of another of Dorchester's notable houses, Cedar Park, whose garden linked through to Trinity Street running parallel to the west. The decorative railings apparently gave glimpses of fine trees and peacocks. Redevelopment of that site in 1895 revealed a beautiful Roman mosaic pavement which can now be seen in the County Museum. Forty years later, a second redevelopment of the same site uncovered Dorchester's famous Roman hoard – a jug, bowl and keg containing more than twenty-two thousand coins dated 257 AD.

The end of the pedestrianised area is marked by the distinctive clock of **Napper's Mite (14).** This almshouse, built in 1615, was for ten 'unmarried men of three score years and upwards'. The street front was rebuilt with a second storey in 1842. Next door was the grammar school founded by another Thomas Hardye (with an 'e'). The name is perpetuated in the Hardye Arcade which leads through to the main central car parks.

If you look across South Street at this point, you will see two plaques high on adjoining buildings. One recalls that Thomas Hardy, author, worked there as a pupil to architect John Hicks from 1856 to 1862. The second marks the home of William Barnes, poet, from 1847 to 1862. The two remarkable men remained friends throughout their lives.

The old line of the Roman walls crosses the end of South Street in South Walks. The war memorial stands on the left and from there the road leads east to Fordington.

Notice the Victorian pillar box, pictured left. It is one of the oldest still in use.

The Weymouth road leads south, past the brewery, railway station and Fair Field where cattle have been penned and auctioned since 1877. This is still the location of Dorchester's Wednesday market which brings coach-loads of tourists into town, particularly throughout the summer months, although cattle auctions have ceased.

A diversion down Weymouth Avenue to **Maumbury Rings (15)** is worthwhile. This Neolithic site was probably used for worship rather than as a settlement. The Romans raised the level of the enclosing banks to form an amphitheatre then, after nearly 1,000 years, it again came into its own as a Civil War defensive position for the Parliamentarians. It has remained a place of great gathering from Victorian days and, from time to time, hosts live theatre in the open

On the way to the Rings the yeasty smell from the brewery might tempt you in for a visit. The Green Dragon Brewery began in Acland Road one hundred and fifty years ago under the capable and redoubtable Sarah Eldridge. It was bought by the Pope family in 1861 and moved to

The bandstand in the Borough Gardens

Weymouth Avenue in 1879, where new premises were built in 1922. Dorchester beer, quaffed in the eighteenth century by 'the late Czar, the Kings of Prussia and Denmark, as well as his late and present Majesty of Great Britain' is described by Thomas Hardy in *The Trumpet Major* as 'full in body yet brisk as a volcano'.

From Maumbury Rings, retrace your steps to the junction of South Street and Weymouth Avenue. Join the main walk where it crosses into Trinity Street. Just inside on your left is Bowling Alley Walk, continuing the line of the Roman defences.

This pleasant, shady path leads to West Walks and the **Borough Gardens (16)**, which were laid out at the end of the 1890s. The colourful Hansford Clock was made by the Lott and Walne foundry, referred to in the Mill Stream Meander. The bandstand is often used for concerts in the summer and, increasingly, other events throughout the year such as a Christmas carol service and a Teddy Bear's Picnic bring residents and visitors to the Gardens.

Leave by the gate at the top of West Walks and cross Princes Street towards Top o' Town. Here on your right is the only remaining section of **Roman wall (17)**. It was given to the town by Lucia Catharine Stone who lived at 40 High West Street, now solicitors' premises.

At Top o' Town, west along the Bridport road, is the imposing bulk of the **Keep Military Museum (18)** which contains information on the Devon and Dorset regiments as well as providing a stunning high-level view over Dorchester.

Top o' Town back to the Town Pump is covered in the Colliton Walk so return along Princes Street past the County Hospital, now being phased out following the construction of a new hospital on the Bridport Road.

Cross over at the junction with Trinity Street by the Tourist Information Centre. Antelope Walk, with Teddy Bear House, will return you to South Street and your starting point.

The Keep Military Museum.

4 FINDING FORDINGTON

St George's Church, overlooking Fordington Green.

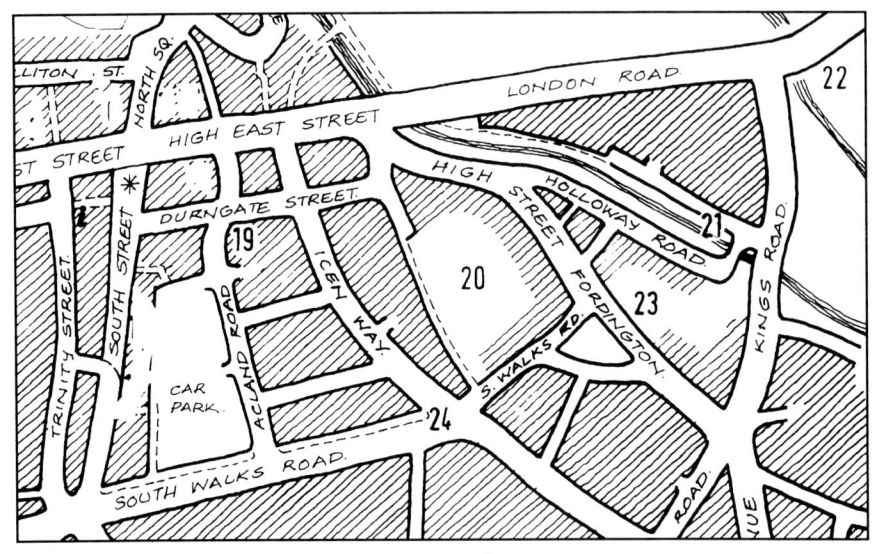

FINDING FORDINGTON. Start from the ✶. Numbered points of interest are:
19 Wollaston, (now Agriculture) House. 20 Salisbury Fields. 21 Prince's Bridge.
22 Grey's Bridge. 23 St George's Church. 24 Martyrs statues.

AS a present day 'suburb' of Dorchester, Fordington retains a character of its own and provides an interesting walk. Leave the Town Pump behind you and walk a short distance down South Street, to Durngate Street on your left. This is an attractive, narrow way with a few specialist shops and makes a quiet route through to Fordington.

At the first junction with Acland Road stands an attractive brick-fronted building, now a suite of offices. **Wollaston House (19)** was a fine residence with acres of gardens stretching back to South Walks. When the gardens were sold for redevelopment, excavations disclosed the remains of Dorchester's Roman baths. They were carefully covered again once they had been photographed and recorded and it is hoped that, like the Town House, they can be opened up again at a later date when funds permit.

Wollaston House was named after Judge Charles Byam Wollaston, who presided at the trial of the Tolpuddle Martyrs. The building was renamed Agriculture House in the early 1990s when it became offices for the National Farmers Union; still, perhaps, a tenuous link with the Tolpuddle Martyrs.

At Durngate Street's second junction – with Icen Way – is the only museum in the country devoted to dinosaurs. It is small and crammed full of interest. Children especially enjoy getting to grips with the computers and hands-on displays.

On the corner of Salisbury Street, the third junction, stands the Salvation Army Chapel. A Roman mosaic pavement in geometric design and dating from the fourth century, was uncovered here in 1905. It can now be seen in the Dorset County Museum. To your right is the entrance into **Salisbury Fields (20)**, which is the way you will return.

For now, turn left for about fifty metres and then right into Fordington High Street. Note the old Dorford (so called because it served DORchester and FORDington) Baptist Church, now Kingdom Hall, built in 1830. Baptisms took place in the River Frome, near the White Hart. The present Dorford Baptist Church stands at Top o' Town.

Continue along Fordington High Street where the metal railings edge the pavement. Fifty burials dating from Roman times were found when, in 1838, the level of the High Street was lowered. These are just a few of the many burials, many of them Christian, found on the outskirts of Dorchester, particularly at Poundbury.

Branch left into Holloway Road which leads to Mill Street where, in 1852, just over one hundred tiny cottages held a population of more than six hundred. It was no wonder that typhus, cholera and smallpox were rife in those days of poor sanitation and open sewers.

Holloway Road gives an elevated view of the mill stream as well as splendid views across countryside to the north of town. Go down the steps and cross the mill stream to Mill Street, now neat with small blocks of flats, continuing to **Prince's Bridge (21)** and the old mill.

It is worth seeking out the two black and white bridge plates. On Prince's Bridge one warns about its use by 'ponderous Carriages'. If you walk a short distance north along the edge of the playing fields you will find the second. It threatens transportation for anyone who vandalises **Grey's Bridge (22).** The Portland stone blocks to this bridge at the eastern entrance to town are beautifully laid and, one would think, an excellent example of undisturbed eighteenth century workmanship. In fact the bridge was dismantled in 1927 to allow road widening. The rebuilding accurately reflects the craftsmanship of the original, stones having been carefully numbered to ensure correct positioning in the 'new' bridge which is scheduled an Ancient Monument.

Retrace your steps over Prince's Bridge and return along Holloway Road as far as Pound Close. This leads left to **St George's Church (23)**

Prince's Bridge and the converted mill at Fordington.

which dominates Fordington village green. The church began life about one third its present size and was drastically enlarged early this century in a manner not to everyone's liking. Thomas Hardy walked off site when changes of which he disapproved were made to the tower.

Over the south door, which is a modern replacement, a Norman panel shows William Belet and his squire on their knees in thanksgiving, as St George rides in to rescue them from the Saracens. The old south door, studded with the date 1717, can be seen in the porch. Restoration work on St George's uncovered footings of possibly a Saxon church and also a remarkable Roman tombstone. The inscribed marble slab is now on the wall of the inner tower.

Among the old graves in the churchyard is that of Nat Seal, a sheep drover who died in 1887. Nat was an unmistakable figure as he went about his work in his cotton smock, always with his favourite Dorset horned ewe, Caroline, by his side.

On leaving the church, cross the green to South Walks. Bear right to the junction with Icen Way and find the **bronze Martyrs statues (24)** by Dame Elisabeth Frink. This vivid group, commissioned in memory of those who died through religious persecution in the sixteenth and seventeenth centuries, occupies a former site of the gallows. Just before the Icen Way junction is one entrance into Salisbury Fields, which provides a lovely walk back to Salisbury Street, Durngate Street, South Street and the Town Pump.

5 ON THE EDGE OF TOWN

THERE are several places to visit just a few minutes away which play an important part in Dorchester's history.

Maiden Castle

The hill-fort where it all began. Take the Weymouth road out of town and turn right several hundred metres past the traffic lights at Maumbury Rings. It is well sign posted and there is car parking. There are information boards at several places on the hill-fort, which provides marvellous and far-reaching views of the countryside as well as the county town.

Thomas Hardy's Cottage, Higher Bockhampton

Thomas Hardy was born in this simple thatched cottage on the border of heath and forest, at Higher Bockhampton. The cottage is now owned by the National Trust and visits to the interior can be made daily, Fridays and Saturdays excepted, between 11am and 5pm, from around the beginning of April to October. For exact dates telephone 01305 262366. The surrounding heath and woodland is covered by waymarked paths. Leave Dorchester over Grey's Bridge to the east and, at the first roundabout, take second left past Kingston Maurward College. The turning to the cottage is on the left just a few minutes past the college and is well signposted. It is about ten minutes walk from the car park.

Max Gate, Hardy's home in later years

Max Gate, just outside Dorchester on the A352 Wareham road, close to the Trumpet Major pub, is named after the nearby toll house Mack's Gate. The house was designed by Hardy who lived there from 1885 until his death in 1928. Now it is owned by the National Trust and an appointment must be made with the tenants, Mr and Mrs Andrew Leah, on 01305 262538. The dining and drawing rooms are open, from April to September, on Mondays, Wednesdays and Sundays from 2pm to 5pm.

St Michael's Church, Stinsford

Leave Dorchester as for Hardy's cottage. Stinsford church is signposted to the right just before the entrance to Kingston Maurward College.

Note: In High West Street, a short distance away from St Peter's Church, is a National Trust shop from which further information about the properties is available. The Tourist Information Centre in Antelope Walk will also be happy to help with inquiries.

MUSEUMS AND PLACES TO VISIT MENTIONED IN THE TEXT

DINOSAUR MUSEUM 01305 269880
Open 9.30am to 5.30pm every day.
Everything to do with dinosaurs, from life- size reconstructions to skeletal remains. Hands- on displays and computer graphics.

DORSET COUNTY MUSEUM 01305 262735
Open 10am to 5pm Monday to Saturday. There is Sunday opening in July and August. Displays of archaeology, geology, natural history and a reconstruction of Thomas Hardy's study. Writers' Gallery opening July 1997.

ELDRIDGE POPE & Co. 01305 251251
There are open tours of the brewery at 11am and 1pm on Wednesdays for individuals and small groups. Larger, fifteen plus groups, can book morning, afternoon or evening tours, Mondays to Fridays.
Dorchester's real ale brewery has been in existence since the 1800s. Thomas Hardy ale is one of the strongest brews available.

THE KEEP MILITARY MUSEUM 01305 264066
Open 9.30am to 5pm Monday to Saturday. Closed between 1pm and 2pm on Saturdays. Military history, uniforms, medals and weapons.

OLD CROWN COURT AND CELLS 01305 252241
Court open 9am to noon and 2-4 pm weekdays excluding Bank Holidays. Cells open for guided tours 2.15 pm to 4.15 pm Tuesday to Friday. Also 10.15am to 12.15 pm Wednesday only from 23 July to 2 September.

TEDDY BEAR HOUSE 01305 263200
Open 9.30am to 5.30pm every day in summer. Telephone for reduced opening times in winter. Human-size teddy bears to enchant the young at home and in the Old Dorset Teddy Bear factory.

TUTANKHAMUN EXHIBITION 01305 269571
Open 9.30 am – 5.30 pm every day.
The Egyptian boy king's tomb and treasures excitingly recreated.